Albert Frey

Gloria Koenig

ALBERT FREY

1903–1998

A Living Architecture Of The Desert

TASCHEN

HONG KONG KÖLN LONDON LOS ANGELES MADRID PARIS TOKYO

Illustration page 2 ▶ Albert Frey standing in front
of the 1953 "Flash Gordon" bedroom addition to
Frey House I.
Illustration page 4 ▶ Sketch of the 1972 bedroom
addition to Frey House II in Palm Springs

Editor ▶ Peter Gössel, Bremen
Project management ▶ Katrin Schumann, Bremen
Design and layout ▶ Gössel und Partner, Bremen
Text edited by ▶ Christiane Blass, Cologne

Printed in Germany
ISBN 978-3-8228-4883-8

To stay informed about upcoming TASCHEN
titles, please request our magazine at
www.taschen.com/magazine or write to
TASCHEN America, 6671 Sunset Boulevard,
Suite 1508, USA-Los Angeles, CA 90028,
contact-us@taschen.com, Fax: +1-323-463.4442.
We will be happy to send you a free copy of
our magazine which is filled with information
about all of our books.

Contents

Introduction

He was an unpretentious, elegant man who dressed in color-coordinated silk slacks and shirts, stood on his head twice a day, swam often in his pool, and lived to be 95 years old. Albert Frey was the first architect in America to have worked with Le Corbusier, and early in his career the visionary Swiss expatriate wrote to his mentor, "I have the opportunity to practice in the exclusive location of Palm Springs, which extends into the desert at the foot of a mountain range not far from Los Angeles. A winter resort for the elite in business, industry and the intellect, it provides the rare pleasure of combining a magnificent natural environment with being a center for interesting and varied activities. Moreover, the sun, the pure air and the simple forms of the desert create perfect conditions for architecture."

It was in response to these particular conditions that Frey assembled a brand new type of architecture, based in Bauhaus, Corbusier, and the International Style, but expanded over his long career to embrace new, free-wheeling adaptations to the exigencies of Southern California living. He used steel, glass, aluminum and the desert landscape itself to create an aesthetic that was entirely his own. He tracked the sun's trajectory during daylight hours and calculated how the rays strike the earth in relation to specific geographical locations. He studied the wind, the rain, and all of the natural world around him and devised a way of indoor/outdoor living that fulfilled the unique requirements of an open and arid landscape, designing hundreds of Palm Springs homes and landmark buildings that have since become exemplars of mid-century Desert Modernism.

It began with his father, who longed to be an architect but dutifully went into the family business instead. Albert Frey Sr. joined his grandfather's successful lithography and printing business along with his brothers and became its creative director, but his interest in architecture never waned and eventually was fulfilled through his son. "He talked to me about it constantly," Frey said of his father's obsession with architecture, "and in a sense he coaxed me into it."

Albert Frey Jr. grew up in Zurich, Switzerland near Lake Zurich and the foothills of the Alps, where he often went boating and hiking with his family. He was born on October 18, 1903, to Ida and Albert Frey, both of whom were involved in the arts, his mother as a musician who taught and gave recitals and his father as an enthusiastic painter of oil and watercolor landscapes. The family had a keen interest in literature as well and it was a tradition to gather together after dinner to read the classics. The Frey household was located near the Frey business so that the intricate technology of the printing press was always in the background of their lives.

As a young boy Frey's first architectural project was a teepee he built with his playmates for games of cowboys and Indians. He also built a series of canoes with bentwood frames and stretched canvas, experimenting with materials until the canoes were waterproof and could be taken out successfully on Lake Zurich. He used reeds from a nearby pond to build playhouses in the summer and igloo-type huts in the winter. The nascent architect liked to work with his hands and showed an early mechanical skill

At Le Corbusier's atelier in 1928: Albert Frey (center) with Le Corbusier, Nikolai Kolli, P. Naham and Charlotte Perriand

that would serve him well in his career, progressing from blocks, erector sets and tinker toys to building crystal radio sets, electric motor kits and model airplanes. He also had an uncanny ability to accurately draw whatever constructions he visualized in his mind.

In the fall of 1921, at the age of eighteen, Frey enrolled as an architectural student at the Institute of Technology in Winterthur. His father had studied art at the Institute and found the instruction to be practical and pragmatic. Albert had first looked into the University of Zurich, but it was a four-year curriculum instead of the three offered at the Institute and considerably more costly in the long run. Frey felt that the Institute of Technology offered a more fundamental approach to basic architectural design, with classes in engineering and construction, advanced mathematics, mechanical and free-hand drawing, watercolor rendering, and the principles of structural, mechanical and electrical engineering. The Institute was an hour's train ride from Albert's home in Zurich and for the next three years he used the travel time to study and review his classes. During summer vacations he apprenticed in the architectural firm of Arter & Risch in Zurich, learning practical skills that included masonry, pouring concrete, building walls, and supervising construction on urban housing.

Frey received his degree in 1924, and although he felt that his training at the Institute of Technology was thorough in traditional construction he wanted to broaden the scope of his formal education to include some of the modern methods and materials being used in contemporary design. He read avidly about the Bauhaus school in Germany, the De Stijl movement in Holland and the new modernism developing in Brussels, where he would later work. Current architectural periodicals such as the German *Wasmuths Monatshefte* and the Swiss *Werk* described the innovative and original work being done by Walter Gropius, Ludwig Mies van der Rohe and Le Corbusier. He also saw the Wasmuth portfolio of Frank Lloyd Wright and was inspired by the American architect's inventive use of the modern idiom. In Erich Mendelsohn's *Amerika* and Otto Wagner's *Moderne Architektur* he studied the industrial materials such as corrugated metal, structural steel, and reinforced concrete that were to become the basic building blocks of his design.

After graduation Frey embarked upon an extended vacation in Italy, traveling by train to visit historic centers such as Florence and Venice, studying and sketching landmark buildings along the way. In a series of drawings of the buildings in the Piazza San Marco, in which he omitted all of the elaborate and superfluous decoration, Frey focused on the basic components of structure and space. The drawings once again reflected his interest in the spare simplicity of modern construction. Once back in Zurich the young architect realized his opportunities were limited to the traditional style of architecture practiced there, a style that was a reflection of the conservative Swiss persona, but anathema to Frey's progressive sensibilities.

While trying to decide how to proceed with his life Frey read an issue of *Werk* that focused on the modern architecture being built in Brussels, Belgium, and decided he would see it for himself. He found it was possible for a German Swiss national to get a visa and work permit in Brussels, both of which were not available in France, which was his first career choice. French was the principal language used in Brussels and Frey decided to seek employment there and prepare himself for the time he would be eligible for a work permit in France. In 1925 he traveled to Brussels where he contacted modernist architect Victor Bourgeois, and although Bourgeois was not hiring at the time he recommended Frey to his colleagues Jean-Jules Eggericx and Raphaël Verwilghen.

When Frey showed them his portfolio of drawings and sketches he was hired on the spot. He moved into a boarding house in the Boitsfort suburb and settled down to work.

In response to the urgent need for housing in Belgium after World War I the firm of Eggericx and Verwilghen was involved in cooperative housing and urban planning, and on the boards were two major housing complexes similar to projects Frey had worked on in Zurich as an apprentice for J. Arter. He was assigned to finish detailing for the Logis and Floréal housing complexes at Boitsfort, both of which were modeled after Dutch and English garden city plans. He also worked on the firm's Fer à Cheval government building design.

His unflagging interest in all things modern led him inevitably to French architect Le Corbusier, first his *L'Esprit nouveau* magazine and then his architectural manifesto, *Towards A New Architecture*. Frey was greatly impressed with Le Corbusier's approach to structural design and his unique ability to articulate modernist thought and explain its underlying methodology. He felt that the book delineated what he wanted to do in his own career and decided that his next goal was the atelier of Le Corbusier. He worked in Brussels for two years and in February, 1927, returned to Zurich where he moved back into the family home in order to save money for his next destination, Corbusier and Paris.

In Zurich he worked in the office of Leuenberger und Flückiger, once again doing construction drawings and detailing as he had in Brussels, but this time for the more conservative type of cooperative housing the firm was producing. The work was undemanding and he found time to focus on the personal development of his own burgeoning ideas, designing and drawing innovative buildings such as A Factory of Steel and Glass and Concrete Parking Tower, and entering a competition titled "Housing For The Old." In 1928 the origins of his future oeuvre were made manifest in the "Minimal Metal House," an early example of affordable housing for the general public. Efficient and compact, the house was clad in what was to become Frey's signature material, corrugated metal.

Design for a washstand in minimal size and for easiest cleaning, entry for a furniture competition in 1928

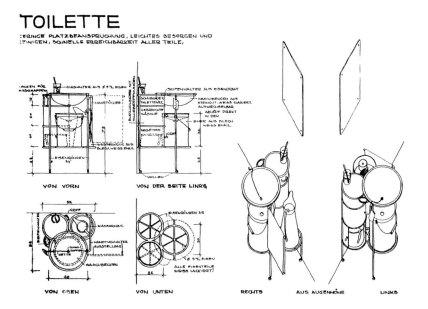

In October 1928 Frey entered France on a student visa and on the morning of his arrival went directly to Corbusier's establishment at 35 rue de Sèvres to apply for work. Le Corbusier, who painted at home in the mornings, wasn't there but his cousin and partner, Pierre Jeanneret, interviewed Frey and said the magical words, "We could use you." He offered him work as a 'student,' which complied with Frey's student visa, at the atelier. He, along with most of the other young architects in the office, would not be paid but would have the opportunity to work with Corbusier. Similar to Frank Lloyd Wright's use of student 'disciples' at Taliesin, the arrangement was considered a privilege and Frey was elated to be hired.

Later that day, around noon, Corbusier strode into the office with bicycle clips on his pant legs having ridden from home on his bicycle, met and talked with Frey and examined his drawings, and approved his cousin's decision to engage him. After a discussion with Corbusier and Jeanneret of his past experience and future duties Frey left to find lodgings, which he accomplished that same afternoon, in a cold-water attic room on the 6th floor of a boarding house. It was close to the office and cheap, a major factor to be considered since he would be living in Paris solely on his savings.

After a few months the quality of Frey's work and his value to the firm became apparent. He was putting in full eight-hour days and often working evenings as well, and it was decided that he would receive a small salary to keep him going and to pay for his minimal needs. He was working with Corbusier and absorbing his principles by what Frey termed "osmosis," a dream he had conjured into reality. Corbusier would arrive at the atelier at noon, commenting and exchanging ideas with each of the staff as he strolled around the office examining their progress on various tasks. Frey was in awe of the originality of his numerous ideas and the two men developed a tacit rapport that was a kind of shorthand between them.

Soon he was assigned to work with Corbusier on his first major project in the office, the Centrosoyus Administration Building. Designed to house 2,800 offices, the Centro-soyus was a commission won in an open competition presented by the Soviet government. When the huge complex was finally built in Moscow several years later the plans had been considerably modified, and it was the last modern building Stalin allowed in the USSR. Frey worked closely with Corbusier on the project, focusing on technical renderings and drawing the various elevations of the multi-storied center.

Corbusier's concept for the overall design of the renowned Villa Savoye was a revelation for Frey and he considered his work on it to be the most significant contribution he made while at the atelier. He found the design of the Villa Savoye to be a progressive, carefully devised plan that integrated many of the individual features that made up the International Style, and he was enthusiastic about his participation in the project. He prepared many of the design details for the built-in cabinetry, the windows and sliding doors throughout the house. One of the details he devised was the hardware for the track of the living room's sliding glass doors, which he adapted from a copy of *Sweet's*, an American hardware catalog that featured items being produced in the US that were not yet available in Europe. He also worked on the construction drawings for the house, including some for an unbuilt dog kennel adjacent to the Villa Savoye's Gate House.

Around this time the Cité-refuge of Paris commissioned Corbusier to transform the *Asile Flottant*, a World War I reinforced concrete barge, into a shelter for some of the city's indigent homeless, many of whom lived under the bridges along the Seine. Fre

Albert Frey and A. Lawrence Kocher in New York City, 1932

found the unusual project to be an interesting challenge and worked on the construction drawings, plans and sections for the unique housing for the homeless. Frey was involved in much of the work in the atelier and felt that he was enriched by the proximity to Corbusier and the experience of working closely with a leading proponent of the International Style. But as summer approached and the work load in the office diminished dramatically Frey realized he could soon be out of a job and in July 1929 he regretfully resigned, although he maintained his friendship with Corbusier over the years to come.

After a six-week vacation with his family at their summer retreat on the Riviera, Frey returned to Brussels in October of 1929 where Eggericx and Verwilghen rehired him at a good salary to serve as the firm's chief designer. He had applied for a visa to America while still at Corbusier's atelier and began to save the necessary money to emigrate when he received it. Living frugally, he worked diligently during the day and attended school to study English at night. When his visa came through he booked passage on the German ocean liner Bremen, and in summer 1930 took the next step to fulfill his personal dreams by exploring the exhilarating technological frontiers of America.

The young man from Zurich arrived in the United States on September 5, 1930. Frey was prepared for his new adventure with a list of New York modernist architects he had found in *Werk* magazine and contacted all of them upon his arrival. At the office of A. Lawrence Kocher he found that Kocher's previous associate, Gerhard Ziegler, had just returned to Europe, leaving him shorthanded. A. Lawrence Kocher, was an MIT-trained New York architect and managing editor of *Architectural Record*. Frey showed Kocher his portfolio of architectural drawings and sketches, and their excellence, combined with the fact that he had recently worked with Le Corbusier, led to his being hired as Ziegler's replacement. Kocher hired him at a salary of twenty-five dollars a week, a very generous sum in those depression years, as well as room and board with the Kocher family at their home in Forest Hills, Long Island. In addition to his practice, Kocher was managing editor of *Architectural Record*, a prestigious magazine read all over the world, and felt that Frey's language skills in German and French would be of value in future issues.

"From the very beginning Kocher and I were interested in prefabricating houses," Frey said of their partnership in an interview with *Architecture d'Aujourd'hui* magazine. "We wrote articles together about methods of construction, and we also made many proposals for houses to standardize and prefabricate." Affordable housing was modernism's holy grail at the time and the idealistic notion of using modern technology to provide good design as well as shelter was the genesis of Aluminaire House, the building that was to bring the firm of Kocher & Frey international recognition.

In September 1930, the same month Frey began work at the small firm as associate architect, Kocher was invited by Allied Arts and Building Products to design a building for their annual exhibition in 1931. With Gerhard Ziegler he had designed the previous year's entry, a fully furnished and equipped modern architect's office that had been very well received by the general public, and the group asked him to come up with another winner. Presented in conjunction with the Architectural League Exhibition, the yearly event was held at the Grand Central Palace, a massive exhibit hall in New York.

Frey and Kocher were both interested in low-cost housing and decided to present a prototype of an economical single-family dwelling that would showcase some of the innovations available in modern technology. Using a quarter-inch scale model to

Ralph-Barbarin House near Stamford, Connecticut, 1932, with A. Lawrence Kocher

convince suppliers of its worth, Frey enlisted such companies as Bethlehem Steel, Pittsburgh Plate Glass, Alcoa, and Westinghouse to donate supplies and services to the venture.

The resulting Aluminaire was the first of its kind in America, a steel and glass structure clad in sheet aluminum that reflected Frey's work on the Villa Savoye with Le Corbusier but was a true original in concept. The house became the star attraction, drawing thousands of visitors and substantial press coverage, with commentary running from the ridiculous to the sublime. The cutaway cube structure was admired for its futuristic ambience, but the majority of visitors felt the modern house was too austere and lacked the comfortable familiarity of more conventional housing.

In 1932 Aluminaire was chosen by curators Philip Johnson and Henry-Russell Hitchcock as one of only six buildings from the United States to represent the modern movement in America for the Museum of Modern Art's prestigious "International Exhibition of Modern Architecture" at the Grand Palace in New York. The show featured early modern buildings from all over the world and traveled across the country for two years, educating and influencing the public about the modern idiom. All of this was documented in *Architectural Record* and within a year of his arrival in America Albert Frey had made a name for himself within the architectural community.

Despite this early success, Kocher did not have enough work to keep Frey busy and the office solvent. It was the midst of the Depression and clients were few and far between. In July, 1931, Frey arranged to work part time for William Lescaze, a fellow Swiss architect who had graduated in Zurich a few years ahead of him, and continued as a designer at his firm until July 1932. In January 1933 Frey returned to Zurich, Switzerland in response to his eldest sister Ida's request to design and construct a modern-type house for herself and her family. The finished house was a three-story, flat roof structure with ground floor piloti that embodied some of the ideas and innovations Frey had learned from Corbusier.

Frey returned to New York in the spring of 1934, and began work on the Kocher Canvas Weekend House, built for his partner, Lawrence Kocher. Based on earlier plans for an Experimental Weekend House, the design reflected Frey and Kocher's keen interest in the possibilities of prefabricated housing. Canvas for the outside walls of the house was donated by the Cotton Textile Institute, and Frey made daring use of the fabric on the floors and to sheath the entire exterior. The three-level house was constructed in Northport, New York and remained viable, in spite of its flimsy cladding, until it was demolished in the 1950s by a developer.

The commission that changed the Swiss architect's life came that summer, when Kocher, who was involved with his work as editor of *Architectural Record*, offered Frey the job of designing a dual use office/apartment building for his brother, Dr. J. J. Kocher. To be constructed along North Palm Canyon Drive in Palm Springs, the Kocher-Samson Building was the project that would bring Frey not only to the California desert but also to his destiny. This building was the genesis of what would become known as Desert Modernism, a unique regional vernacular designed in response to the parameters set by the natural environment. In his 1939 book, *In Search of A Living Architecture*, Frey said, "Plants and mountains, with their curved and irregular contours, create and welcome contrast to the rectilinear practical house form." He applied this principle to all of his subsequent work in Palm Springs, designing a wide range of structures that included commercial and civic buildings as well as residential homes, using his singular style of contemporary architecture set against the stark background of the desert landscape.

The Aluminaire during reconstruction on Central Islip Campus in 1991, with A. Lawrence Kocher

Although he had driven across country in 1932 to visit Frank Lloyd Wright at Taliesin West and stopped in Los Angeles to see some of the work of Richard Neutra, Rudolf M. Schindler, and Julius Ralph Davidson, Frey had never traveled as far as Palm Springs. When he arrived in the fall of 1934 to begin work supervising the construction of the Kocher-Samson Building, he found that the desert and its surrounding snow-capped mountain ranges reminded him of Switzerland and he experienced an immediate affinity for the region that was to become his home for the next sixty-four years.

After the Kocher-Samson Building was completed Frey stayed on in Palm Springs. There was no work in New York with A. Lawrence Kocher and the two friends agreed that it was best to dissolve their partnership. Although they had only designed four buildings together their contribution to modernism in America was significant, and the informative articles they collaborated on for *Architectural Record* had international impact. They teamed up briefly one more time in 1938.

Frey's next associate was John Porter Clark, a graduate of Cornell University and one of the first architects to practice in Palm Springs. Because neither architect was licensed all of their work as Clark and Frey was under the name of Van Pelt and Lind, an established practice where Clark worked previously that allowed them to use their firm name for their commissions. From 1935 to 1937 they completed eight projects, all of them on a minimal budget, with wood-frame construction, stucco exteriors, and lath-and-plaster interior finishes. Wherever possible Frey glazed the exterior, installing sliding doors and metal-framed windows into his designs. During this time Frey focused on the modern commissions while Clark took the more conventional work, a division of labor that kept the office busy and financially viable.

The Guthrie House, one of the eight houses Albert Frey built in collaboration with John Porter Clark, was part of the Purdue University Housing Research Project's "Portfolio of Low-Cost Houses," a study of nine houses that were currently under con-

Farmers' Market construction, Palm Springs, 1947

struction at the time that focused on ways to reduce manufacturing costs in anticipation of producing mass housing. The project was organized by members of the building industry as a practical study of construction methods, using the latest materials and techniques available. Specifications were designed by participating architects and industrial engineers to fit the needs of the average prospective home buyer, and to provide houses that could be built at an established price of $5,000 maximum limit, a sum that in 1935 was a considerable amount of money.

Clark and Frey's house for Mr. and Mrs. James V. Guthrie was designed to fulfill the requirements of the "Portfolio of Low-Cost Houses." It was economically built to withstand the fierce sun and arid climate of the desert using the venerable adobe house as a model for its stucco exterior sheathing and flat composition roof covered with gravel. The roof had galvanized iron flashing at copings and a slight pitch toward drains. The house was of wood frame construction and faced south, and the south wall of the living room was made entirely of metal-framed sliding glass doors that were protected by aluminum-faced curtains and a large retractable awning made of canvas. Windows had steel casements with crank operators and were backed with bronze screens. The end walls of the plan's projecting wings were windowless for privacy. Frey's exterior color scheme of sage and green walls in the patio area to avoid glare and warm white on the rest of the house to provide heat reflection was the result of careful study of the site and its orientation to the sun.

The interior floor plan was well-organized and efficient, with the kitchen and laundry in the right wing, a living and dining room in the center, and two bedrooms with a bath in between making up the left wing. In the living room the fireplace was centered on the north wall with dining furniture to one side and a built-in couch and desk on the other. The cement floor was covered with blue linoleum, while walls and ceiling, which were stucco over plasterboard with a smooth trowel finish, were painted pale yellow. The woodwork and built-in furniture were an eggshell color and the curtains and cushions blue. The bedrooms had built-in storage spaces which were also

The office building of Clark and Frey on North Palm Canyon Drive in Palm Springs, 1947

painted eggshell, and the walls, ceiling, and bedspread were blue. The final cost for the house, incredibly cheap in today's terms, was three dollars a square foot for all work in the general contract, including built-in furniture and cabinets, but excluding floor covering, gardening, and architect fees.

Although the office of Clark and Frey was solvent during the next few years, the commissions they received were increasingly for traditional houses more in the style of John Porter Clark. When Frey was contacted by Philip L. Goodwin in 1937 and asked to come to New York and work as a designer on the Museum of Modern Art building he decided it was an opportunity he had to take. He had worked on various tentative plans for the Museum in 1933 while he was a part-time employee for William Lescaze and was familiar with the project. Goodwin and Edward Durell Stone had been awarded the commission by MoMA and wanted Frey to help with design modifications and additions. When he arrived in New York in May, the Museum was already under construction. During a two-year period Frey worked on detailing and design modifications of the glass-walled streetside façade and designed a 600-seat lecture hall and a reading room.

In 1939 Goodwin offered Frey a full partnership, but when he called John Porter Clark in Palm Springs to tell him the news, his former associate informed him that he had received his California license and needed Frey's help with the new commissions that were coming in. Clark counter-offered with a full partnership in what could now be the official firm of Clark and Frey which Frey accepted, driving across country in a 1938 Ford convertible coupe back to the desert and the snow-capped mountains he would never get out of his blood.

"The California desert continues to charm me," Frey said in his series of letters to Le Corbusier, "...continues to nourish me, to give me an opportunity for modern architecture... It is a most interesting experience to live in a wild, savage, natural setting, far from the big city, but without losing contact with civilization." Palm Springs was a small village then with most of its streets unpaved until it was incorporated as a

The apartment complex Villa Hermosa in Palm Springs, 1945–1947

city. The main boulevard of North Palm Canyon, destined to become the downtown thoroughfare, was widened to accommodate commercial buildings, and Clark and Frey were commissioned to design and build several of them along both sides of the street. A typical Clark and Frey project, including their own office complex, was a rectangular building, one or two stories high, with a flat roof and corrugated metal paneling for walls. Painted off-white or beige, these sleek structures set a modernistic ambience that greeted visitors as they drove into the city of Palm Springs from the drab approach of the highway. Located at the base of the San Jacinto Mountain range, the city was a glorious blast of color in the sparkling desert air, with skies that were brilliant blue in the daylight and black velvet and star-spattered at night.

Known as "The Playground of the Stars," Palm Springs had been a favorite resort town for the Hollywood elite since the 1920s, many of them, including Clark Gable, Greta Garbo, Cary Grant, Lucille Ball, and Frank Sinatra, buying homes in the area as a desert retreat. The movie crowd congregated at silent-screen star Charlie Farrell's Racquet Club, where Frey built guest cottages along the stream that flowed through the grounds as well as a new cocktail lounge and dining room, which was filled most nights with a star-studded crowd of revelers from the entertainment world. Over the years the city became the home of several United States presidents including Dwight Eisenhower, John F. Kennedy, Ronald Reagan, and Gerald Ford. A two-hour, 125-mile drive from Los Angeles, Palm Springs was also attractive to tourists, who not only wanted a vacation in the sun but the opportunity to glimpse firsthand some of their favorite celebrities from the silver screen as well as from the White House. Although

John Porter Clark and his wife Louisa in front of Frey's own guest house

primarily a winter resort, the city became a year-round retirement community as well in the 1970s and 1980s, and by the 1990s became popular with a new group of younger urbanites looking for homes in the Desert Modernism style.

In 1940 Frey bought a two-acre parcel of land on Via Donna adjoining El Mirador with a panoramic view of the desert landscape and the nearby mountains surrounding it. He drew up blueprints for a small experimental house that embodied the principles he outlined in his book, *In Search of A Living Architecture*. For Frey House I he used materials to create a plan that was crafted for the desert, with several wall planes extending beyond the house's footprint into the raw natural terrain beyond. In 1947 he added a large living room and although the original house already had a swimming pool he built a smaller second exterior/interior pool that meandered into the new room. The famously round "Flash Gordon" second story bedroom with its eight port-hole windows was added in 1953. Frey sold the property in 1960 and the final owner-developer tore down the signature house to make room for a subdivision that never came to pass.

Motorists driving through the windy stretch on Highway 111 that leads into Palm Springs are greeted at the northern entrance by Frey's Tramway Gas Station, a futuristic structure with a canopy 'flying wedge' roof that spans 95 ft. and is supported by six steel pipe columns reminiscent of Corbusier's piloti. A gateway to the Palm Springs Aerial Tramway, and located at the bottom of a slope of Mount San Jacinto on Chino Canyon Road, the building was commissioned by the City Council who wanted something spectacular to attract tourists to the town and to the Tramway. Frey was involved

Library in Banning, 1954–1955

in the early planning stages of the Tramway itself, traveling to Switzerland to consult with experts in overhead cable carrier design. In 1963 he designed the Tramway's Valley Station, a bridge-like building constructed of steel trusses, that spans a shallow stream and is anchored to outcroppings at either end. The legendary Tramway Gas Station has endured a troubled history, marred by graffiti and neglect and threatened with demolition before the city of Palm Springs finally bought it in 2002 and converted it into a Visitor's Center.

In 1963 Frey built what is considered an enduring masterpiece of Palm Springs architecture, a house with a rock that runs through it perched 200 ft. above the city on rugged mountainous terrain. Frey turned a liability into an asset, wrapping his steel framed and glass-walled house around a massive boulder situated at the northeast corner of the property, using it to serve as a partition between the living and sleeping areas. Presented with the plans, City Hall officials were skeptical about Frey's unconventional design, but knowing his solid reputation in the city they allowed him to proceed. In 1972 he added an extension including a bedroom on the western side of the house. Frey lived the rest of his life in the small, jewel-like structure on Palisades Drive, high on a mountainside reminiscent of the Alps.

During the sixty-four years the Swiss expatriate lived in Palm Springs he imprinted an entire town's architecture with Freyness. Beginning with the Kocher-Samson building in 1934, he created a life work in the desert that included the Raymond Loewy House, the Guthrie House, the Clark and Frey Office Building, the Aerial Tramway and Gas Station, Palm Springs City Hall, the Desert Hospital, the North Shore Yacht Club at Salton Sea, Villa Hermosa, the Première Apartments, and his famous Frey House and Frey House II. Over the years he designed a series of elementary schools for the Palm Springs Unified School District, utilizing his spare, modern style to construct school buildings that were practical, functional, and cost-effective. The flexible open plans were configured to accommodate further expansion and to keep up with future community growth.

Desert Hospital in Palm Springs, 1950–1952

Throughout his career in the desert Frey designed numerous houses and additions at Smoke Tree Ranch, an exclusive resort community of sprawling, ranch-style homes reminiscent of the early 'prairie' designs of Frank Lloyd Wright. Although he often had to adapt his modernist approach in order to conform to the Ranch's guidelines and building codes, his architecture always maintained its integrity. Semi-retired from the late 1960s, Frey continued to enjoy a long and fulfilling career as a practicing architect.

In the spring of 1990 most of Frey's personal papers were acquired by the University of Santa Barbara Art Museum for its Architectural Drawing Collection. An exhibition titled "Albert Frey: Modern Architect" was organized by author Joseph Rosa and opened at the Art Museum in 1992. It traveled to two other venues in the United States, three in Europe, and to the Palm Springs Desert Museum with Frey in attendance. In 1995 the exhibition was shown in Frey's native Switzerland. In the 1990s Frey became something of a star architect, with media shoots at Frey House II and features on his work appearing in *The New Yorker*, *Wallpaper*, *Forbes*, and *Elle Décor*. It was a renaissance he lived long enough to experience. He passed away at home of natural causes on November 14, 1998, and is buried at the Welwood Murray Cemetery in Palm Springs. Frey House II was bequeathed to the Palm Springs Desert Museum along with a selection of photographs and personal papers.

1930–1931▸Aluminaire

Syosset, New York ▸ with A. Lawrence Kocher

Roof terrace of the Aluminaire on the location in Syosset, Long Island, 1932

Designed for the "Allied Arts and Building Products Exhibition" held jointly with the 45th Annual Architectural League Exhibition at the Grand Central Palace in New York City, on April 18 through April 25, Aluminaire was the only full-scale building in the exhibit. The three-story aluminum, glass and light-steel house was calculated to fit within the limitations of the hall's atrium space and was constructed in less than ten days. An experimental showcase for modern technological materials, it was a proto-typical single-family home that could be easily and economically replicated for mass housing.

Frey began by making a quarter-inch scale model of the proposed building. He carried the intriguing model around in a box to show to suppliers such as Alcoa, Westinghouse, Bethlehem Steel, Pittsburgh Plate Glass, and the Aluminum Company of America, all of whom donated standard mass-produced building materials and services in exchange for the advertising and publicity the venture would bring. The arrangement was an opportunity for these companies to demonstrate to the public how their latest products could be utilized to manufacture a low-maintenance house for modern living, and allowed Frey and Kocher free access to the industrialized materials they required. Alcoa was the largest donor, providing the columns, beams, girders and the exterior panel cladding for Aluminaire.

The three-story steel-framed structure was sheathed in narrow-ribbed aluminum panels backed with insulation board. The windows and door frames were of steel and the pressed steel flooring layered with insulation board and black linoleum. The ground level served as a carport, and had a furnace room, an entry, an open-air porch and a stairway. The first floor was a two-story living room 17 ft. high, with a dining room, a master bedroom and bath, a kitchen, and a stairway. A built in glass and metal cupboard concealed an extendable dining room table specifically designed by Frey for the space. The floor above had the library, a bathroom and a spacious rooftop terrace to provide additional living space.

One of the most unusual problems of construction was how to anchor the house's six supporting columns without setting them in concrete. The dilemma was solved by attaching flanges and bolting them to the exhibition hall floor. The pipe columns bore a similarity to Corbusier's piloti, and Frey readily acknowledged his mentor's influence on Aluminaire and its similarity to houses Corbusier had done for a 1927 exhibition in Stuttgart. Only five inches in diameter, the aluminum pipe columns supported the house's two elevated levels.

The Aluminaire was the first house of its kind, and the first structure designed by a disciple of Le Corbusier to be constructed in the United States. It was a forerunner of the "House of Tomorrow" exhibits featured at the 1933 Chicago and 1939 World's Fairs. Frey and Kocher published an article in *Architectural Record* titled "Real Estate Sub-divisions for Low Cost Housing" to coincide with the event and to clarify their views. People flocked to the Exhibition, 100,000 or more according to newspaper accounts, but the public response was mixed, as reflected in the following reviews at the time:

Opposite Page:
Overall view of the Aluminaire at the New York Institute of Technology's Center for Architecture on the Central Islip Campus Pipe columns similar to Corbusier's piloti are five inches in diameter and support the house's two elevated levels.

The Aluminaire in Syosset, Long Island, 1932
Aluminaire was dismantled and moved from the exhibition hall and reconstructed by Wallace K. Harrison.

First and second floor plans

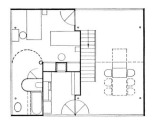

"I saw the 'zipper' house at the architectural show. Its real name is Aluminaire, but having learned that one of its virtues is speed of erection and demolition, promptly decided that the former name was more appropriate. So 'zipper' it was, all last week, to the crowds who never wearied of climbing its stairways, poking through its rooms and hanging around to discuss it." Deems Taylor in *The Brooklyn Eagle*.

"Now for the 'canned house'! The latest thing in architecture! When a man resides in one of these things he is practically living in a metal container. If father wants a new door cut through to his room he doesn't get a saw. He gets a can opener." Review in the *New York Times*.

Frey later commented, "People don't like technology for their own houses; they always have some traditional style in mind... I felt that the thing to do was to make technology aesthetically attractive so the public would accept it. I always felt that structure came first."

In 1932 Aluminaire was included as one of the few examples of American architecture in the Museum of Modern Art's "International Exhibition of Modern Architecture," curated by Philip Johnson and Henry-Russell Hitchcock, and was simultaneously published in their influential book, *The International Style*.

When the exhibition closed it was announced that a New York architect, Wallace K. Harrison, had bought the Aluminaire for $1,000 and intended to move it to his eleven acre estate in Syosset, Long Island. Harrison, known for his work in many large public projects, including Rockefeller Center, the United Nations Building and Lincoln Center, wanted to relocate the house on his property and use it as a weekend retreat. Aluminaire had been designed for mass production, with components that could be taken apart and transported easily. The plan was to dismantle it, mark the pieces, and reassemble it like a jigsaw puzzle at its new location. Although the house was taken apart in only six hours it took more than ten days to put it back together, because the sections had been shipped to Long Island and then left out in a heavy rainstorm that washed away all of the identifying chalk marks. It was finally reassembled on the property with only a few pieces left over.

Since then the Aluminaire has had a harrowing history. In 1932 Harrison designed and built on a large addition for his family that severely altered the original concept. In the 1940s the house was moved again, this time to a new location on Harrison's property that placed it up against a hillside. The pipe columns were removed and the ground floor, including the garage, entry and utility room, became a basement, and new entrances were cut into the house's next level. When Harrison died in 1981 the estate was sold and the Aluminaire, which had been deteriorating for the previous forty years, became a rental property and was further altered.

In 1986 the owner evicted his last tenant for non-payment of rent, and then applied for a permit to demolish Aluminaire House and subdivide the property into four parcels. At this point architect Joseph Rosa, who at the time was researching the work of Albert Frey for a book, discovered the pending demolition and joined forces with the

The Aluminaire in Syosset, Long Island, 1932
Both the corrugated Sheathing and the triangular reinforcing metal sheets are clearly visible.

Ground floor plan

Huntington Historical Society and state and local preservationists to protect the house and secure its future. After a concerted campaign to publicize the situation in the media, including a report in the *New York Times* stating that "an icon of modernism was poised for extinction," the New York Institute of Technology offered to move the house to its Center for Architecture in Central Islip, Long Island with the intention of using it as a museum.

A restoration grant of $131,000 was obtained by the school in 1987 from the Department of Parks, Recreation and Historic Preservation, to cover part of the cost of relocation. At this point the Aluminaire's owner came forward and donated the house to the school. For the moving process, it was decided that architecture students would record and dismantle the house piece by piece. Using existing drawings and photographs to document the original design, the components were meticulously numbered for future re-assembly and then moved from the Harrison estate and stored in a warehouse at the New York Institute of Technology Central Islip campus by 1989. Over the ensuing years architecture faculty and students reconstructed the house to near-completion, but in 2003 NYIT closed the Architecture Program at Central Islip and Aluminaire once again became a house in search of a home.

1934 ▸ Kocher Canvas Weekend House

Northport, New York

The generously glazed living room

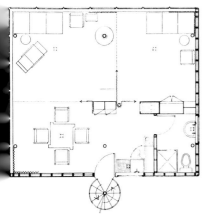

Plan of the upper floor

In 1934 the New Uses Section of the Cotton Textile Institute contacted A. Lawrence Kocher at *Architectural Record* to suggest joining forces to publicize cotton as a viable alternate material to use in the construction of small, low-cost houses.

Frey had experimented with cotton canvas when he was a boy. During his teens in Zurich, he was a member of a rowing team and on occasion rowed on the lake until dawn with his friends. One of his hobbies was the fabricating of canoes made of bent wood frames and canvas. He built several of these sleek craft, including one in his friend's basement that was so big that once it was finished they had to remove the door to get it out and onto the water. He applied this early experience in Switzerland to design with Kocher two houses, the Experimental Five Room House and the Kocher Canvas Weekend House, to be used by the Cotton Textile Institute as prototypes to promote the commercial use of canvas for the building industry.

Both houses were similar in plan and both had flat roof decks that could be used for living arrangements. Fireproof cotton canvas was used on the exterior and dyed canvas on the interior. Experimental Weekend House was built on steel columns raised high enough to allow a carport underneath and had a living-dining-sleeping room with kitchenette and bath at the second level. The Experimental Five Room House was raised only 2 ft. above the ground and featured a long narrow deck and a stairway off the front of the house. These houses never progressed beyond the model stage but they served as a proving ground and provided the catalyst for the 1934 Kocher Canvas Weekend House.

The canvas-wrapped house under construction

Built for Frey's associate A. Lawrence Kocher on a coastal site in Northport, Long Island, the house made full use of the technological know-how acquired on the previous two unbuilt prototypes.

Kocher Canvas Weekend House had three levels. The ground floor was a carport and porch. The middle level was enclosed, and access to it and the floor above was by an exterior spiral staircase. Living amenities were all on this second floor and drapes were used to divide the space into bedrooms at night. The top level was a roof deck used for sunbathing or outdoor sleeping. Interior walls and ceiling were covered in plywood veneer and the floor in canvas. The Cotton Textile Institute donated all the canvas for the house to test its weather resistance and durability when exposed to the natural environment.

On the outside walls of the house heavy duty canvas, waterproofed and fireproofed, was stretched tightly over diagonal redwood sheathing. Just before the canvas was applied the redwood was coated with white paint to act as a bonding agent between the two materials. The canvas was applied horizontally starting at the bottom of the wall until the entire house was wrapped in the experimental material. Finally it was painted with three coats of oil-based paint followed by a finish coat. On the exterior the pipe railings, the piloti, and the canvas roof deck were painted sage green and the steel sash windows and awning a deep red.

The house had three levels; the ground floor was a carport, the middle level was enclosed and the third level was a roof garden.

Although the Kocher Canvas Weekend House withstood a fierce hurricane that destroyed all the trees around it in 1938, it became clear over the years that canvas couldn't compete with the more durable industrial materials being developed by modern technology. In 1950 Kocher's canvas house on Meadow Glen Road was demolished by a developer.

1934–1935 ▸ Kocher-Samson Building
Palm Springs, California ▸ with A. Lawrence Kocher

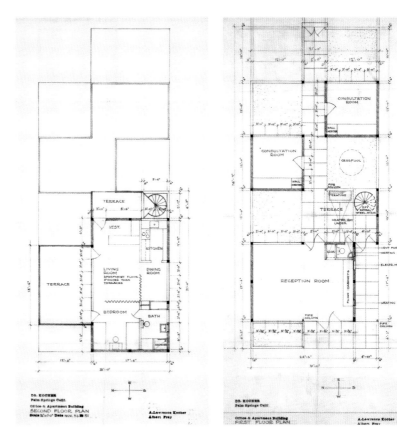

The plans of second (left) and first (right) floor show the concept of the enclosed patios sitting side by side with the cubic rooms in the back.

Albert Frey drove in 1934 from New York to Palm Springs to supervise the construction of the Kocher-Samson Building, commissioned by his partner's brother Dr. J. J. Kocher, who held the distinction of being the first doctor to practice in Palm Springs. The building at 766 N. Palm Canyon Drive was to be a dual-use two-story structure with offices on the first floor and an apartment above. Although Palm Canyon Drive was the main thoroughfare in Palm Springs, which was known as "the village" at the time, the street was still an unpaved dirt road in 1934 with few buildings along its path. The long, narrow site for the Kocher-Samson building was surrounded by open desert, and realizing that the land would be developed and occupied in the future, Frey designed the building to look inward, with offices interspersed with courtyards, patios and decks.

A series of stepped-back cubic forms with an integral modularity, the Kocher-Samson was a radical departure for its time and place. For the first floor Frey used a poured-concrete post-and-beam system with concrete block infill for the walls. The plan was based on a 3 x 3 grid and divided into solid and negative volumes; indoor and outdoor geometrical squares and rectangles with a large reception room and indi-

The series of stepped-back cubic forms had an integral modularity.

The apartment on the roof cantilevered over the entry forming an overhang to shade the offices below.

vidual offices enclosed with a high perimeter wall. A central, covered, circulation pathway ran the length of the first floor space.

The perimeter walls of the second floor were lightweight pressed-steel frames prefabricated in sections at the factory and assembled and welded on site. The apartment was entered via an open, spiral staircase, and the terrace was enclosed with matching pipe railings, both of which were to become signature elements in Frey's later work. Inside was a vestibule leading to a large rectangular space divided into living, sleeping and dining areas with an enclosed kitchen and bathroom. The apartment was placed at a ninety-degree angle forming overhangs to shade the offices below. The outdoor terrace was covered with four-inch metal decking, as were all the floors and roofs of the building.

A year later, in October 1935, the Kocher-Samson Building was included in the New York Museum of Modern Art exhibition titled "Modern Architecture in California". Other architects featured in the show were Richard Neutra, Rudolf M. Schindler, William Wurster and A.C. Zimmerman, and the inclusion of Frey's work in the prestigious exhibition was a noteworthy accomplishment. The catalog described the Kocher-Samson Building as being "typical of the restrained ingenuity of the Eastern experimentalism which in contrast with that of California seems economical and chaste." In other words, International Style was morphing into Desert Modernism in the work of Albert Frey.

1940 ▸ Frey House I
Palm Springs, California

On the west side, the deep overhang provides sun shelter for the car.

Opposite page:
Albert Frey sitting on the terrace on the east side of his house

"I am thrilled every day by the varying spectacle of the natural views that are part of it, changing with light and color, wind, rain, stillness, and sunshine," Albert Frey told *Progressive Architecture* in a 1948 article about Frey House I. "I believe, however that a full understanding of this type of house will come only gradually because most people's reflexes are conditioned by the conventional, closed-in houses in which they have grown up."

Frey House I was anything but conventional and it was as much an aberration in Palm Springs in 1940 as Aluminaire had been in New York in 1931. The only modern buildings in the Coachella Valley prior to Frey House I were Rudolf M. Schindler's Popenoe Cabin in 1922, Frank Lloyd Wright's Oasis Hotel in 1923, and Louis Sullivan disciple William Gray Purcell's house in 1933; all the rest were Spanish, Victorian or variations of adobe boxes. Frey's spare, minimalist structure set down amidst the cactus

Indoor and outdoor areas work closely together for Frey's ideas of modern living.

and tumbleweed in the wilderness of the desert landscape was a juxtaposition that was either jarring or beautiful, according to the eye of the beholder.

Frey had been living in the back room of the offices of Clark and Frey when he found a two-acre parcel of land on Paseo El Mirador adjoining Via Donna and decided to buy it and build his own home. He set the house well back into the widest portion of the deep triangular lot with an orientation that presented an endless view of the desert scene and the 10,000 ft. high San Jacinto Mountain range beyond. Experimental in design, the small, flat-roofed house was based on the principles presented in his 1939 book, *In Search of A Living Architecture*, and Frey conceived of it as a model for future prefabricated and mass-produced homes.

The house was a single volume 16 x 20 ft. rectangle with one room for living and sleeping. The small kitchen and bathroom had built-in case work and plumbing in a common wall. The standard wood frame construction was sheathed with corrugated aluminum on the exterior and asbestos cement board tinted pale pink and green on the interior. The corrugated metal ceiling was painted blue. The simple structural system was laid out on a modular basis both in plan and section, using 4 x 8 panels to sheath the wood. The aluminum was applied vertically to the perimeter walls and

The pool was added later by Frey and surrounded by his typical concrete outdoor furniture.

Wing walls extended beyond the house into the desert landscape.

Left:
View from the kitchen to the pool

Opposite page:
A round patio table was suspended from the ceiling with aluminum wires.

horizontally to the building's extended wall planes and roof overhangs. These materials were fastened to the wood frame with screws, and Frey applied many of these pre-fabricated panels himself while supervising construction.

Wing walls, "walls that go out and make spaces within the landscape," as Frey explained to an interviewer, were a direct continuation of interior walls that extended beyond the house and created small terraces for outdoor activities on the desert floor. He acknowledged the influence of Mies van der Rohe's Barcelona Pavilion as the inspiration for this architectural element. The roof plane was designed with deep overhangs to provide wind protection and shade for the pool pavilion and a carport. A pioneer in indoor-outdoor design, Frey used aluminum-framed floor to ceiling windows and sliding glass doors with sliding screen panels to open the front of the house onto the patio, the pool, and the wide vista beyond. A series of brilliantly conceived flat concrete slab seats, some covered with colorful cushions, defined the sculptural landscape surrounding the pool.

Environmental controls, before the advent of refrigerated air-conditioning, were fundamental and designed for Frey's year-round living in the desert. The metallic cladding of the house reflected some of the fierce heat of the daytime sun. Circulation depended on the adjustment of the sliding glass walls and was supplemented with a cooler unit that washed, dehumidified, and fanned the air in the hot Palm Springs weather. The unit was suspended from the roof, just outside the corrugated metal kitchen

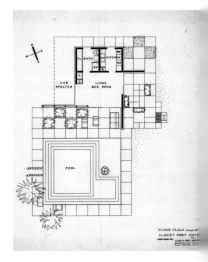

Floor plan

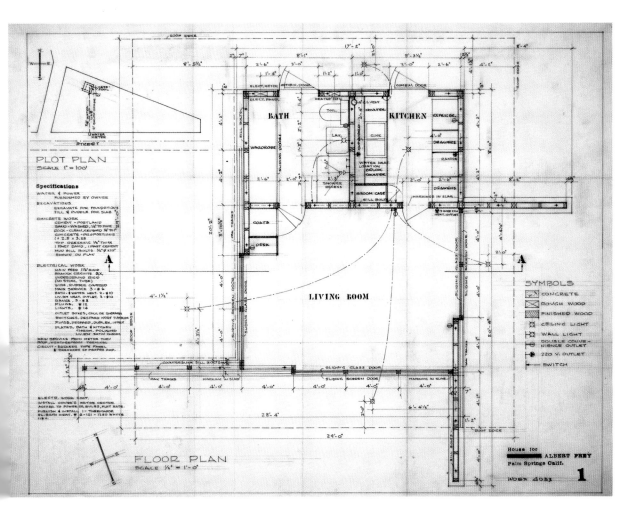

Working drawing with plot plan and specifications

wall. When it was cool electric space heaters inside the house provided warmth, as did the natural solar benefits of the glass walls on the south, east and west perimeters.

A small, one-room guest cottage was built on the acreage in back of Frey House I, and Frey's widowed father came from Switzerland in the last few months of his life to stay with his son, using the cottage as an art studio to paint the snow-capped San Jacinto mountains so reminiscent of his native Swiss Alps. Over the years the cottage was put to good use for Frey's visiting friends and business associates, including Richard Neutra, his wife Dionne and son Dion, and legendary architectural photographer Julius Shulman, his wife Emma and daughter Judy.

A 4-page spread in the Italian magazine *Domus* featured the house in 1945, giving Frey's work international acclaim. Frey lived in and studied his house in relationship to

the environment, thinking of new ways to improve on his original concept. In 1948 he added another large living-sleeping area with a skylight over the bed to view the stars and a folding partition to seal it off from the rest of the house. The focal point of this new addition was a small, curved interior/exterior pool, similar to one he designed in 1946 for the Raymond Loewy House. This second pool had corrugated metal sides, a fountain, a stepping stone bridge, and a lushly planted solarium garden with a wild grape vine that climbed up and entwined itself in the crevices of the indoor ribbed-aluminum ceiling. The solarium area and the new living-sleeping room were enclosed within a surrounding curvilinear wall of corrugated plastic panels of translucent red and yellow fiberglass. A special idea was realized with a suspended dining table and a trapezoidal trellis surrounding the pool.

View over the pool in the countryscape

Top:
A skylight over the bed to view the stars was part of the 1948 addition.

Bottom left:
A lushly landscaped indoor pool meandered into the living area.

Bottom right:
Frey sitting at his tiny workplace

1941–1955 ▸ Elementary Schools
Cathedral City, Needles and Palm Springs, California

Opposite page and right:
Vista Colorado School in Needles, California, 1948

Cahuilla School in Palm Springs, California, 1941, with John Porter Clark

When Clark and Frey were asked by the Palm Springs Unified School District in 1940 to design an elementary school for the small farming community of Cathedral City, Frey used his desert expertise to plan a simple and rational schoolhouse that was modern in concept, economical in design, and answered the needs articulated by the school board client.

The original school, before a series of additions, was a small, flat-roofed, stucco-clad building with one classroom and bathroom facilities. Cathedral Elementary School was the first school building for the firm of Clark and Frey and led to many other commissions throughout the Coachella Valley.

The next school project was the 1941 Cahuilla Elementary School in Palm Springs, named for the Agua Caliente Band of Cahuilla Indians, and situated on a large, flat site with potential for future expansion. Clark and Frey designed a multi-stage scheme that was flexible and could be enlarged as needed to keep pace with community growth. The innovative plot plan was a progressive vanguard of future school design and along with Neutra's 1930 Emerson Junior High School and Kump and Falk's 1941 Carmel Woods School, became a prototype for elementary schools all over the country.

The rectangular building contained three classrooms and was connected to an adjacent small bathroom facility by a cantilevered roof overhang that shielded the classrooms from direct sunlight. The resulting covered corridor served as a walkway for the children and provided shade and shelter. Clerestory windows oriented to the south afforded natural light and ventilation. Classrooms had built-in cabinetry inside and outdoor work areas in the corridor with storage cabinets and sinks.

**Katherine Finchy School in Palm Springs,
California, 1948–1949**

The primary requirements of children were the parameters of the design. Successive stages of construction, throughout the 1940s and early 1950s, adhered to the original system, adding classrooms, a kindergarten with a separate playground, an administration building, an arts and craft building, and a cafeteria. Recreational facilities for Cahuilla Elementary included baseball diamonds, basketball courts, and ample space for other outdoor activities on the school ground's sprawling desert acreage in the southern part of town.

In 1948–1949 Clark and Frey built their largest school, the Katherine Finchy Elementary School at 77 Tachevah Road in the north section of Palm Springs. Based on the same expansion system as Cahuilla Elementary, the Finchy School was designed to allow for future growth that would match the burgeoning population in the Coachella Valley since the end of World War II. The first stage of the overall plan consisted of four classroom buildings, a kindergarten, an administration building and a cafeteria. The flat-roofed structures were connected by covered passageways and ramps were used in the corridors to accommodate the slight slope of the natural terrain.

A large outdoor assembly area with two classroom wings on each side and the administration building situated to the east were surrounded by wide covered corridors. As at Cahuilla Elementary, the wood-frame structures were built on concrete foundations for economy, with pipe-column supports, aluminum roof-flashing, and corrugated aluminum on the outside corridor ceilings. At strategic outdoor points areas of wire-glass partitioning was used to alleviate the strong northwest winds.

Katherine Finchy School in Palm Springs, California, 1948–1949
Covered corridors served as walkways for the children and provided shade and shelter.

Interior color schemes were Frey favorites; sage green, pale yellow, and dusty rose alternated on classroom walls. Exterior plaster wall surfaces were painted light buff with contrasting light gray trim. The administration building was a terra cotta color. Water evaporative blower units, the most economical system available at the time, cooled the classrooms and natural gas furnaces supplied the heating through a forced air system distributed by overhead ducts. Completed in early 1959, the school's construction costs were calculated at $ 9.50 a square foot for the finished areas, with open corridors figured at half the price.

The firm (Clark and Frey, as it was known until 1952 when the name was changed to Frey and Chambers to include Robson C. Chambers as partner) developed a reputation for creating rational, economical and environmentally sound schools, and designed or altered several including Vista Colorado Elementary in Needles, California, 1949; "D" Street Elementary School, addition in Needles, 1949; Essex Elementary, addition, Needles, 1949; Cielo Vista Elementary School, Palm Springs, 1955; Nellie Coffman School, Multi-Purpose Room and addition, 1958–1960; Palm Springs High School, Shop Building, 1958; and Palm Springs High School, alterations, 1961.

1945 ▸ Hatton House
Rancho Mirage, California ▸ with John Porter Clark

The site plan for the Hatton House project shows two separate houses divided from each other by a natural desert arroyo and oriented so that the living room of each is angled to the southwest with a view of the mountain range and the desert sunsets. This unusual layout was requested by the client, an entertainment industry executive who wanted a place to relax on the weekends and a guest house that he could use as a rental to defray some of the expenses so that eventually the project would pay for itself.

Clark and Frey were commissioned to design a two-bedroom main house, a one-bedroom guest house, and a shop far in back of the property for power, laundry equipment, a workroom, and a caretaker's quarters. Frey used 4' x 8' modules of standard panel board throughout the project, a construction material that provided quick assembly and was easily adaptable to future changes and additions. The houses were wood frame, with exterior walls of corrugated metal with aluminum paint. The roofs were aluminum foil between two layers of asphalted felt. For cold nights there was electric radiant heating, and cooling in the heat of the day was provided by evaporative units situated on the roof.

Although the two houses were very similar in plan and volume, they differed in that the main house was an expanded rectangle and the guest house a geometric square. Both the two-bedroom main house and the adjacent one-bedroom guest house had built-in circular fireplaces in the corner of the living room, with wide sliding glass door units on either side that framed the desert landscapes outside. The fireplaces were faced in brick with flagstone hearths, and the floors were a troweled cement finish on concrete slab. Interior walls were asbestos-cement wallboard and the ceilings were painted corrugated metal. Flush chrome lights inset in the walls were used throughout.

Each house had chimneys at the corner and a southwest-facing terrace defined by wing walls that reached into the desert to provide windbreaks and extra living space. Aluminum paint was used on both corrugated and smooth metal exterior surfaces to reflect the heat of the sun and to supplement the evaporative cooling units on the roof. The corrugated metal ceiling plane and the asbestos-cement-board walls were painted variations of pale yellow and green to replicate the desert foliage and the window frames were painted terra cotta.

Entrance side of the guest house
The interiors were painted in bright yellow and green.

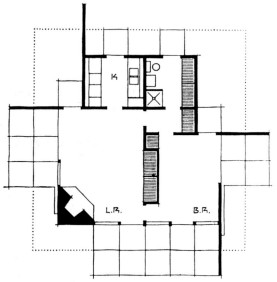

Floor plan of the guest house

Cowboy actor Raymond Hatton and his wife, Frances in front of their house on the outskirts of Palm Springs

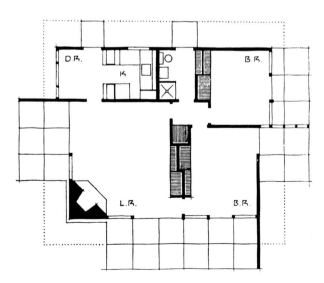

Floor plan of the main house

1946–1947·Loewy House
Palm Springs, California

In 1946, while Richard Neutra was building his iconic Kaufmann House, Frey began construction on the Loewy House. Both projects were in the Little Tuscany area of Palm Springs and were on continuous lots. Neutra often stayed in Frey's guest cottage and the two architects shared the same contractor on their construction sites. Raymond Loewy had commissioned Clark and Frey to build a bachelor pad in the desert where he could relax after his frequent worldwide travels. His hobby was collecting houses, and he already had a hunting lodge, a resort house on the Riviera and Sands House at Sands Point, Long Island, but this time he wanted to start from scratch and build one of his own.

Loewy was a world renowned industrial designer and creator of famous logos that dated back to the 1920s including such icons as Coca Cola, Exxon, Frigidaire, Lucky Strike, Air Force One, and NASA's Skylab Space Station. He came to America from Paris, France in 1919 after World War 1 with only his French Army uniform on his back and forty dollars in his pocket. He began his career as a designer of window displays for Macy's and Saks Fifth Avenue and then became a fashion illustrator for *Vogue* and *Harper's Bazaar*. By 1929 he had opened the design firm that was to become one of the most famous and successful in the world.

Loewy wanted the house, which he called "Tierra Caliente" (warm earth), to be a small, compact vacation house that could be overseen by one servant, and found a suitable property that measured 180 by 330 ft. on Panorama Road. Covered with large

Entrance seen from outside

The living room with the entrance area in the background
A desert boulder and a portion of the pool extend into the room.

The living room with the kitchen in the back
A pathway of champagne-colored brick was inset at the juncture of the boulder.

boulders and indigenous cactus, the rocky lot was an interesting challenge to Albert Frey, who worked within its natural parameters to create a footprint that incorporated all of the aesthetic possibilities. As a result, Julius Shulman's photographs of the finished house are breathtaking from all angles, with the deconstructed desert and manmade architecture coalescing into art.

The L-shaped plan is rational and spare, made up of two long rectangular wings at right angles to each other that enclose a kidney-shaped swimming pool shaped by the location of the surrounding boulders. One of these desert boulders, along with a portion of the pool, extends a few feet into the living room of the house, and Frey designed a clear plastic insert that can be fixed below water level to seal the room completely. The outdoor/partially indoor pool, ahead of its time, had submarine lighting and filtered, constantly flowing water. Thirty-foot long sliding glass doors moved toward the center and rested on the pool boulder to enclose the living room. When the doors were open the pool had a removable guard rail. The bedrooms, along the other flank of the house, opened directly to the pool and patio area, which had an open latticework ceiling.

Set on a poured concrete slab, the house consisted of a foyer, living room, two bedrooms, bathroom, kitchen and a single servant's room. The foyer and living room were carpeted to the edge of the pool, and a pathway of champagne-colored brick was inset at the juncture of the boulder. Matching this was a champagne brick corner fireplace,

The trellis around the kidney-shaped pool framed the magnificent desert landscape

Raymond Loewy

with an amoeba-shaped stone from the Salton Sea hanging above it. Pecky cypress, a wood favored by Loewy, was used extensively for interior walls and for a geometric grid inset with glass squares against the exterior bedroom walls. A redwood trellis framed the view around the free-form pool and featured a large palm tree casually growing through one of the squares. Two poles supported the trellis with a sheet of corrugated glass between them serving as a wind break. Mexican glass bottles, souvenirs of Loewy's travels, were filled with pink-tinted water and placed around the pool, where they were illuminated at night with the glowing pool lights. Later, when Loewy married, he enlarged the house to accommodate his wife and daughter, and kept a 1963 Studebaker Avanti, for which he designed the famous logo while in residence at his new desert retreat, parked in the open carport.

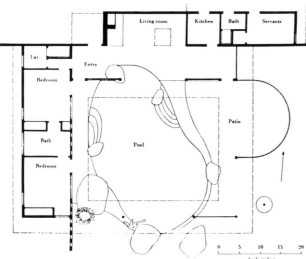

A small grassy patio on the east side of the pool was later filled in with an addition to the house.

Floor plan

1949–1963 Aerial Tramway Station
Valley Station ▸ Palm Springs, California

Historic postcards of the valley station

Opposite page:
The restaurant deck on one side of the gorge

The Aerial Tramway project was conceived by a young electrical engineer named Francis Crocker, the manager of the California Electric Power Company, who came to Palm Springs in 1932 when it was a small settlement in the desert with a grocery store, a bank, a café, and a drug store to serve the population of a few hundred people. These were the years before air-conditioning, and Crocker dreamed of a way to get out of the oppressive heat and up to the snow-capped top of the San Jacinto Mountains that surrounded the town. His idea of a tramway was initially dismissed by local officials as ridiculous, but eventually they formed a Tramway Authority and persisted over the years until they were able to enlist the help of Governor Earl Warner in 1945, who signed a bill authorizing the project. It took sixteen more years for Crocker to make his dream come true by enlisting the support of Governor Pat Brown in 1961, and bonds were finally issued to fund the initial construction phase of the tramway. It was almost 30 years since the time Crocker began his quest, but the long delay proved to be advantageous to the project because of the drastically improved technology that became available for the tramway's extraordinary requirements.

It was decided that the master plan would consist of three major components: the steel carrier cable and passenger cars; the Mountain Station near the top of the north slope of the San Jacinto Peak; and the Valley Station, the passenger terminal on Tramway Road where the ride would originate. Williams & Williams, a prominent Palm Springs architectural firm, was hired to design the Mountain Station and Frey and Chambers were commissioned to design the Valley Station. Frey's former partner, John Porter Clark, was named coordinating architect for the entire project.

The most daunting task by far was building the daring and innovative cable system for the Aerial Tramway. It required the kind of expertise only available at the time in Europe, and the Tramway Authority consulted with several companies there to design a master plan and provide some of the required equipment. Because Frey was Swiss and could speak the language he was selected to go to Switzerland as their representative. He met with executives of Von Roll in Bern, a leading company with years of experience in overhead cable carrier design, to discuss the technical aspects involved. While in Europe Frey visited several operating aerial tramways in Switzerland and the Dolomite Mountains in Italy to observe firsthand their working mechanisms and methods of operation.

The steep, mountainous gorge of Chino Canyon at the northern edge of Palm Springs was chosen as the designated site for the Aerial Tramway project. By the time construction of the first tower began in August, 1962, many changes in the scheme had taken place. Technical advances and the availability of heavier track cable made it possible for the vertical ascent to be made in a single rise, and a midway transfer station was eliminated from the planning, reducing the number of towers from nine to five. Each of the five remaining towers was individually designed to fit on a designated pad in the precipitous terrain. The first tower was built at the Aerial Tramway entrance, four miles up Chino Canyon adjacent to the Valley Station and parking lot, but the other

The sloping roof allowed a gorgeous view of the tramway cars going up and down the mountainside.

four presented unique problems that were eventually solved by the use of a fleet of helicopters.

Helipads were built near each of the tower sites and helicopters made more than 20,000 flights before construction was completed, one of the greatest engineering feats using helicopters ever accomplished. Much of the heavy equipment was disassembled, loaded onto the helicopters, and reassembled at the workplace location by workers who had been flown in. The 29 miles of locked-coil cable required for the tramway was made by the American Steel & Wire Company and delivered to the site by truck. In order to complete installation of these cables a giant hoist with a 100-ton capacity was flown in pieces to the Mountain Station site at the top of the tramway run. The two 80-passenger tramway cars and other necessary machinery were sent from Von Roll in Switzerland, along with an engineering consultant to supervise their correct use.

The problematic site chosen for the Valley Station was necessary in relation to the overall scheme of the Aerial Tramway and was situated over a shallow stream bed that ran down Chino Canyon with mountainous terrain on either side of the open space. The location was actually two sites with a deep gorge between them and required a structure that would span the gap. Frey designed what was essentially a covered bridge, with foundations set on plateaus at each end of the steep canyon walls, and the bridge/building's substantial width airborne over the flowing stream below. Walls of the Valley Station were structural steel trusses with diagonal glazed openings on both sides of the building serving as visitor windows.

The left section of the structure was designed to house tramway equipment adjacent to the cables leading to the upper station, and the right section contained visitor and passenger facilities that included a gift shop, a cocktail lounge, a snack bar, and a

The valley side with the machinery building on the left

observation area. A slightly pitched roof was calculated to allow visitors inside the building to enjoy a panoramic view through the diagonal windows of the tramway cars running along the steel cables through the mountain canyons. On the other side, the windows framed the steep descent of Chino Canyon down to the rocky desert floor of the Coachella Valley below. The Valley Station was flanked by Tower #1 on one side and a stairway leading up from the parking lot area on the other.

The Palm Springs Aerial Tramway was officially launched on October 12, 1963. Governor Pat Brown officiated at the ribbon cutting, and group of celebrities and civic leaders, including the governor and his wife, paid $1,000 each to ride the inaugural jaunt to the top. Today the tramway is one California's tourist attractions, a fifteen minute ride with rotating tram cars traveling from the Valley Station, at an elevation of 2,643 ft. to the Mountain Station, at 8,516 ft. above the Coachella Valley floor. The dramatic difference in temperature between the two ecological zones can be as much as 40 or 50 degrees. At the Mountain Station, located in the 14,000-acre San Jacinto State Park & Wilderness area at the top, an alpine forest of giant Ponderosa pines is often sprinkled with snow, while down below at the Valley Station the sun-baked rocky landscape is typical of its setting in the Coachella Valley, a contrast much appreciated by Swiss expatriate Albert Frey during his years in Palm Springs.

1952–1957 · City Hall
Palm Springs, California

view from the south-east with the two
different roofs over the entrance areas
to assembly and office wings

opposite page:
the view from the east shows the walls
of the assembly room stepping back.

In the early 1950s Palm Springs had outgrown the small wooden building on Palm Canyon Drive that was being used as a City Hall, and the City Council members commissioned Frey and Chambers (Robson Chambers had been made a partner) to design a new facility. The architectural firm had acquired a reputation in the community for achieving excellent modern design that was desert-wise and cost-effective, using industrial materials that required minimal care. A site was chosen on Tahquitz McCallum Way, a wide landscaped thoroughfare that led eastward from the heart of the city to the Palm Springs Airport, in the hub of a proposed Civic Center. The design process for City Hall was a collaboration between the architects and city officials, with council members, structural and acoustical engineers, and the city manager all contributing expertise in their various fields.

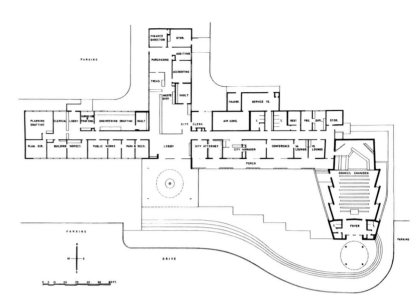

Plan with office wings on the west side and the Council Chamber on the east

Frey used splayed walls and a baffled ceiling to enhance the acoustics in the Assembly Hall.

In July and August 1955, Frey took a break from the intense summer heat of Palm Springs, and embarked on a long-planned trip around the world. After a brief stop in New York, he flew to Zurich where he met up with his sister and her husband and traveled to France to visit two of Le Corbusier's buildings, the church in Ronchamp and the living unit "Unité d'habitation" in Marseilles. His extended tour took him to Rome, Agra, Athens, Cairo, New Delhi, Bangkok, Hong Kong and Tokyo. He renewed two friendships on the trip, visiting Pierre Jeanneret, in Chandigarh, India, and Kunio Maekawa in Tokyo, both colleagues from the time at Corbusier's atelier. Refreshed and invigorated, and inspired by the wonders of the world he had seen, Frey returned to Palm Springs in the fall of 1955 and finalized the plans for the new City Hall.

The entry façade features two striking entrances, one to the main lobby area of City Hall and the other to the adjacent Council Chamber. The main entrance is shaded by a square, free-standing portico with a circular cutout in the center that allowed a flagpole through to fly above the building and was later replaced with a planting area and three tall palm trees. A matching circular canopy of exactly the same diameter as the cutout in the portico marks the entrance to the Council Chambers. This canopy is a poured concrete disc supported on four columns, with a permanent white silica sand finish and engraved with signage stating "The People Are the City." Connecting the Council Chambers to the main building is a covered breezeway embellished with a design motif of alternate vertical sections of shallow, cylindrical, steel sunscreens. Cut at angles to help shield the building and divert the glare of the morning sun, the sheet metal cutouts create an elegant decorative design along the corridor. The perimeter walls of the structure's exterior are constructed of concrete blocks stacked directly above each other in a geometric pattern. The walls are terra cotta and the exterior trim is painted sage green.

Extending from the interior's central lobby corridor are two wide symmetrical wings, one housing offices for the executive staff and the other designated for planning and facilities. The rear corridor leads to space for the city's financial offices and personnel. The City Council Chamber at the right end of the complex was designed as a public

A covered breezeway connects the lobby area of City Hall to the Council Chambers.

The main entrance is shaded by a square free-standing portico with a circular cutout in the center.

assembly hall, and because there was no electrical amplification available at that time Frey worked with consultants to incorporate some of the acoustical engineering skills he had learned from Corbusier, using splayed walls and a baffled ceiling to enhance and distribute the quality of the sound.

The monumental structure of the City Hall complex is the first building seen by visitors coming from the Palm Springs Airport. Over the years of its design and construction it became a joint project of Clark and Frey with Williams & Williams, a respected architectural office in the area. The later expansions, the Civil Defense wing, added to the complex in the early 1960s, and the Engineering wing added in 1985, were designed by the Williams firm.

1953▸Frey House I Remodeling
Palm Springs, California

Opposite page:
The renovated trellis featured a light metal construction with fiber roofing.

In 1953 Frey drastically altered the appearance of the house with a circular second-story bedroom addition that has been famously called the "Flash Gordon" suite, a modification that author Joe Rosa said "transformed the house from a pure Miesian structure to an expressionist one." It was Frey's contention that nothing in the alterations was merely decorative and that everything had a function. The second-floor design was based on a Mayan observatory called the Tower of the Sun that Frey had seen in Chichen Itza, Mexico, and was a round tower with a series of round windows that tracked the outdoor panorama and provided a 360-degree view of the desert landscape and the mountains.

View from the dining area over the pool to the curved fence

The eight porthole windows were each wrapped in sheet metal visors of varying depths adjusted to its location and the angle of the sun. Four of the windows were fixed and four had pivoting glass for ventilation. The tower's exterior was sheathed in em-

The futuristic bedroom suite in the shape of a round tower with porthole windows sits over the living room.

Bottom:
The bedroom interior walls were covered with tufted yellow vinyl fabric.

Top:
The hanging staircase was suspended from the ceiling with aluminum rods.

Right:
Plan

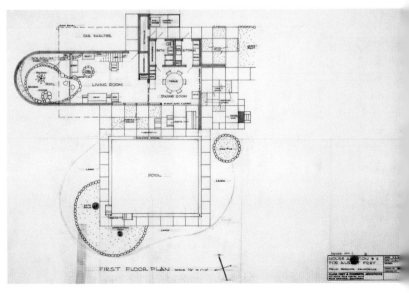

ossed diamond-patterned aluminum. The bedroom's interior walls were covered with
ufted yellow vinyl fabric with floor-to-ceiling drapes of the same material in electric
blue. Ceiling panels were blue perforated acoustic tile. Frey added an innovative and
quite beautiful hanging staircase leading to the bedroom addition that was suspended
from the ceiling with a shining maze of 1/4" diameter aluminum rods.

   Frey sold the property in the 1960s. The final owner-developer tore down the
angular house, replaced it with a traditional stucco box as a model for his project, and
converted the two-acre lot to a subdivision for four sites. However, the venture failed
and the developer, having destroyed what might have become a Palm Springs histori-
cally designated landmark, went into foreclosure.

A curvilinear wall of ribbed fiberglass and corrugated metal enclosed the pool area.

Top and opposite page:
The fencing of the pool area drastically
changed the openness of Frey's desert home.

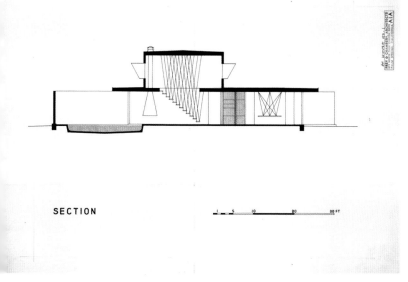

SECTION

Section

1955–1956 ▸ Cree Residence II
Cathedral City, California

The sundeck doubled as a carport below.

In 1947 Raymond Cree commissioned Frey to design the Desert Hills Hotel, a resort complex consisting of a restaurant and a string of nine individual houses sited along his large property on a mountainside. The hotel was never built and in 1955, at the same location as the unrealized project, Frey began construction on the family residence.

Nestled into the scattered boulders at the pinnacle of the Cree acreage, the front façade of the rectangular building was supported on steel piloti that formed a sundeck above and a shaded car port below. A corner fireplace made of indigenous stone anchored the house to the site's rocky terrain.

1957–1958 · Première Apartments
Palm Springs, California

Opposite page:

Each unit had a private balcony that overlooked the terraced pool area.

The Première Apartments complex was quintessentially Palm Springs, a resort hotel positioned on the site to maximize the vistas of landscape and mountains and to minimize the impact of the arid desert climate. Contrasted with Frey's earlier resort endeavors, the San Jacinto Hotel in 1935 and the Villa Hermosa in 1945–1947, which were wood-framed buildings reminiscent of European workers' housing of the 1930s, the Première Apartments project was an evolved and streamlined version of his previous efforts. Frey's clients were admirers of his style and wanted a modern, flat-roofed, two-story structure built on their property on West Baristo Road, located in the heart of the city and only a few blocks from Palm Canyon Drive. They planned to live on the premises as managers of the other units and required a two-story apartment designed exclusively for them at the center of the complex.

The spatial configuration was similar to that of the typical vernacular California roadside motel of the time, an L-shaped plan enclosing a community pool and patio area, but Frey designed the Première to have a view of the mountains from each of the units. The two-story building had a central lobby area with a single line of attached rooms on either side, and entrances to the apartments were along an exterior corridor at the back of the building. Each unit had a private balcony that overlooked the terraced pool area, with vertical dividers separating them with red, green and yellow fiberglass panels. The first-floor patios had a round concrete base surrounded by a planting area and were enclosed with a low, curved panel of white fiberglass. The second-floor units were also enclosed with white fiberglass, which was set within pipe railings covered with yellow fiberglass. Each apartment had an air-conditioning unit installed on the outdoor patio walls.

The pool was surrounded by terraced gardens and a narrow walkway that defined the outdoor landscaped area. Frey designed fixed concrete block seating units, similar to those installed at Frey House I, which were covered with upholstered cushions and fitted with outdoor lighting fixtures for nights around the pool. Parking facilities for the hotel were sheltered by metal roofs to protect the cars from the sun.

The Première Apartments was sheathed in corrugated metal and a startling addition to its sleek exterior was the round windows at each end of the second-story units. Like the windows in his Frey House I "Flash Gordon" addition, they were shaded by metallic cylinders and had the futuristic look that was a part of Frey's architectural repertoire and would be used again in forthcoming structures.

Years later, when Frey found out that the building was scheduled to be demolished to make room for a large development, he was able to save it from being razed. He contacted the new owners of the Première Apartments and with their cooperation arranged to donate the building to the Orchid Tree Inn, located just around the corner on South Belardo Road, in exchange for the cost of removal and relocation. They detached the Première from its foundations, cut it in half, and trucked the truncated building to a prepared foundation on the Orchid Tree Inn property, where it became part of the Inn complex.

View from the parking lot

Section

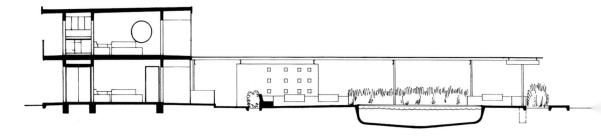

An L-shaped plan enclosed a community pool
and patio area.

1958–1959 ▸ North Shore Yacht Club
Salton Sea, California

The North Shore Yacht Club was to be a fanciful rendition of the ship-in-the-desert image, a jaunty, nautically-styled building set on the northeast shores of the Salton Sea, an inland lake located in the desert wilderness of Coachella Valley thirty miles away from Palm Springs. Albert Frey was commissioned to build the Yacht Club by Ray Ryan, a Texas oil millionaire and owner of the Palm Springs El Mirador Hotel and his partner in the venture, Trav Rogers, both of whom consulted with Frey on the Yacht Club's marine-like design. They had invested heavily in the area, buying up real estate adjoining the north shore of the Salton Sea to develop what they and other speculators foresaw as a Lake Tahoe-like property. They wanted the Yacht Club to be the linchpin of their future development and to represent a winter resort that offered swimming, fishing, water sports and boating to vacationers in the arid wilderness of the desert.

Frey used his personal palette of concrete block, corrugated metal, and aluminum framed glass windows and doors to design a 200-foot long building with a gently curving façade that seemed to push into the water of its Marina setting. The concrete block ground floor was used for dining and social facilities and a curved and suspended stairway, similar to the one used in the Frey House I addition, led to a second floor that cantilevered out over the ground floor and was sheathed in corrugated metal. A central Compass Room Lounge with a large seating area and four round, porthole-like windows looking out on the water, was flanked on each side with outdoor terraces covered with metal awnings that served as observation decks. Metal-clad visors wrapped the four cylindrical windows on the outside. Essentially, the second floor was like a flying bridge, with brightly colored semaphore flags decorating the yellow corrugated plastic railings.

The Yacht Club seen from the waterfront

Bottom:
Plan of the upper floor

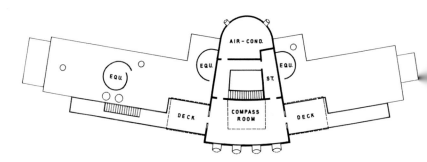

The exterior stairs provide direct acces from the lounge to the marina.

Ray Ryan's celebrity pals were among the first guests at the North Shore Yacht Club, sunning on the beach, racing speedboats on the Salton Sea, and partying at night. Frank Sinatra, Dean Martin, Jerry Lewis and the Marx Brothers were regulars at the Yacht Club in its heyday and the "Lake Tahoe" concept seemed to be working exceptionally well. In 1959 Ryan and Rogers expanded their real-estate holdings, buying a hillside property nearby and naming it North Shore Beach Estates. They subdivided the development into building lots and asked Albert Frey to design a prototype home as a showplace for the project. Although never built, the model house was typically Frey, with wing walls extending into the landscape and concrete block, corrugated metal, and glass windows and doors melding into a desert-wise dwelling. Frey also designed the North Shore Beach Motel across the street from the Yacht Club, but the design was altered during construction and he did not acknowledge it as his own.

Other real-estate investors who had bought into the new utopia at the Salton Sea, built motels, restaurants, beaches and marinas in the next few years, until in the 1960s the fragile environment upon which the entire project was based began to suffer. The problem was that the ecosystem of the Salton Sea was subject to increasing pollution

A pool area merged into the Salton Sea
panorama.

and fluctuating levels of salinity, and when the two hazards reached a critical point th
fish in the artificial lake began dying off, releasing an unpleasant stench into the deser
air that spread across the lake to the surrounding resort communities. Eventually th
polluted water was declared unfit for swimming and the boat races and water sport
came to a halt as well. By the 1970s the once popular vacation destination was turnin
into a ghost town.

These ecological imbalances were the result of an accident in 1905, when poorly bui
irrigation canals bringing water to the agricultural farms of the Imperial Valley from th
Colorado River collapsed, causing a torrential flood that inundated communities, farm
and the main line of the Southern Pacific Railroad. The Colorado River changed cours
and flowed into a large dry crater that was the site of prehistoric Lake Cahuilla. The floo
was finally stopped in 1907 with a strategic line of protective levees built of boulder
dumped from boxcars along the Southern Pacific railroad tracks. At this point the new
inland saline lake was almost 40 miles long and 13 miles wide, encompassing an area c
approximately 400 square miles. It was named the Salton Sea and became a part of th
existing ecology of the Sonoran desert wilderness into which it had accidentally flowe

Bottom:

View from the lounge on the upper floor over the marina

The central Compass Room Lounge was flanked on each side with outdoor terraces that served as observation decks.

In the 1970s the persistent rise in the Salton Sea's water level reached the buildings near the shoreline, flooding the exterior dining terrace of the Yacht Club and lapping at the surrounding structure. The water finally receded and by the late 1980s the Yacht Club was used again as a restaurant. However, a constant fluctuation in water levels caused recurring floods and by the late 1990s the building was boarded up and abandoned. In the ensuing years numerous engineering strategies have been explored to help stabilize the Salton Sea and reach some sort of environmental sustainability, none of which have produced a solution to the region's fundamental imbalances.

1963–1964 ▸ Frey House II
Palm Springs, California

Entrance side with pool and Albert Frey cooling his legs

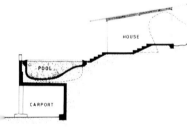

The section shows how the pool cantilevers over the carport.

The rock. The huge boulder that Albert Frey lived with intimately from 1964 until his death was an integral part of his life and his architecture, defining the living spaces of his second house with the ancient language of nature. "The house is firmly anchored to the rock," he said in an interview soon after the house was built. "When I first looked at this property, I saw that the house would have to incorporate this rock." He realized that the structure had to be predicated on the buildable portions of the steep terrain, and designing it around the majestic boulder was the only viable solution to the problem. An added bonus of the plan was the fact that the house would be resistant to earthquakes. "Earthquakes are quite common here and whenever there's a quake the house moves with the rock and there's no damage," he explained. "The reason I know that this rock hasn't moved for thousands of years is because it takes that long for rocks to acquire this brown external color—underneath it is gray granite, it is not this color inside."

Frey House II is situated on a steep mountainside dotted with rocky outcroppings, and at the time it was built it was at the highest elevation, 220 feet, of any residence in the city of Palm Springs. Frey has famously said that after looking up at the mountains for over twenty years he decided it would be nice to live up there. His first house was located on the windy flatland of the city, and he wanted to escape from the constant swirling of fine sand and dust that settled everywhere, including the bottom of his swimming pool. The lot he found high on Palisades Drive was considered unbuildable by the owner, who had tried in vain to configure a satisfactory building pad on the

property. Frey bought the site in 1963 for $30,026 and, serving as his own contractor, spent just $32,621 more on construction. When he submitted his plans to the building department officials at City Hall they dubbed the project as "Frey's crazy house," but knowing and respecting the quality of his work allowed him to proceed.

Frey began by having an accurate survey made, using stakes and strings to get an idea of how the structure would fit into the natural contours of the land. He first constructed a concrete block retaining wall on the south side to house the carport and to support a pool on the platform above. Using a small cement mixer on the property, he personally blended mineral pigment into the cement until he had the exact color he wanted, the pink color of a desert sunset that matched the concrete blocks he had chosen. He used the colored cement and concrete blocks throughout the building process, and took advantage of other low cost, low maintenance construction material that were durable, fireproof, and available in desert pastel colors.

The carport is flush with the access road and a cement stairway leads from the driveway to an upper level platform of poured concrete with a terrace and pear-shaped swimming pool. Shallow steps lead into the pool and around it are Frey's built-in concrete benches for sunbathing. Following the contour of the mountain slope, three more steps lead to the house itself, which faces south and is aligned on the urban grid of the city below. The 800-sq.ft. house is all steel-frame construction with exterior walls of heavy-duty, floor-to-ceiling sliding glass doors and colored corrugated aluminum.

Right:
**Philippine mahogany was used for the built-in
furniture, storage units, and dining table.**

The sloping roof is tilted at the same angle as the site with a generous overhang that shades the long wall of glass beneath it from direct sunlight. Made of Cor-ten, a ribbed corrugated steel material with a baked enamel finish, the roof was installed by the sheet-metal company in a single day. Frey also used this baked enamel finish metal for the ceiling and walls of the house, color coordinating the material in shades of sage green, bronze and blue to blend with the outdoor topography. Because the enamel was baked on at the factory it has never needed to be retouched. The roof's slant accommo dates the massive boulder which penetrates the plane of the glass wall at the northeast corner of the structure. I-beams supporting the roof were anchored to the rock to secure it to the house. In what Frey called 'a good trick,' he custom fit a 3/4" aluminum channel to position the glass panels abutting the rock and filled in the gaps with pieces of colored cement and matching pebbles.

The interior is enclosed on three sides by glazed walls that can be opened to the outside creating a roofed pavilion with panoramic views of the city below. Drapes of pale yellow vinyl with Mylar® lining shield the glass doors. The rectangle of the multi-purpose main room is divided by the integral boulder into living, dining and sleeping areas in one common space. The elevation of the floor changes with the contours of the natural grade and the dining room is slightly raised from the living room. The kitchen, bathroom, and HVAC equipment are to the west and the main room is to the east. The interior wall partitions are made of Philippine mahogany plywood, an inexpensive material at the time that Frey brushed with liquid Cabot stain mixed with white to give a driftwood effect to the finish. The mahogany is also used for the built-in furniture, storage units, and a long, wide dining counter that doubles as a work desk during the day. Kitchen cabinet doors and shelves are made of corru gated fiberglass.

Bottom right:
Plan

Bottom:
Frey's built-in lighting fixtures in the ceiling combined infra-red with normal incandescent bulbs.

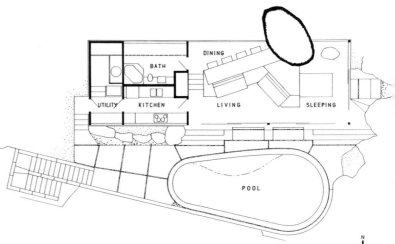

The roof's slant accommodates the massive boulder which penetrates the plane of glass wall at the northeast corner of the structure.

Built-in clock in the living room wall

In 1972 Frey added an extension of compatible design to the west side of the house, with a steel-framed roof and a second bedroom constructed of concrete blocks, enlarging the house to 1,200 sq. ft. Comfortable in the architectural skin of his own design, he lived and worked in his second house for the rest of his life. In an interview when Frey was in his nineties he talked about what it was like to live in such close proximity with the natural world, describing his frequent encounters with squirrels, coyote and quail, and telling the story of a Chuckwalla lizard he befriended. "He was here when I first built the house 30 years ago and is still around. He's very tame and eats little bits of fruit and vegetables out of my hand."

He bequeathed Frey House II upon his death to the Palm Springs Art Museum, with the stipulation that the house would be administered by those knowledgeable about his work and that it would be made available for tours to scholars and architectural students.

1963–1965 ▸ Tramway Gas Station

Palm Springs, California ▸ with Robson C. Chambers

Opposite Page:
Fluorescent lighting illuminated the area around the gas pumps.

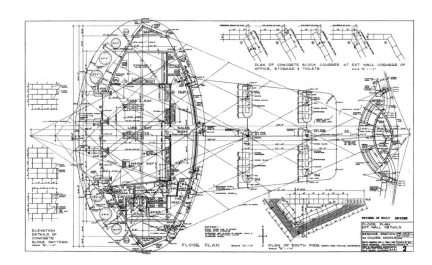

Working drawing

The City Council members wanted a symbol, an audacious and eye-catching structure to inform vacationers that they were about to enter the city of Palm Springs. They also wanted it to be modern, so in 1963 they contacted the firm of Frey and Chambers (John Porter Clark had left in 1956) to design a gateway to the city on land contiguous with the road leading up to the new Palm Springs Aerial Tramway. Frey had designed an earlier set of entry gates, constructed of curving native stone, in 1940 at approximately the same location and they were to be replaced with the new structure.

What he gave the City Council was a prescient example of a biomorphic building, an innovative design inspired by nature. "You have to have your fantasy going," Frey once explained to an interviewer. "After all, that's what life is. When you think what nature produces in fantastic forms, in birds and animals—that's where creativity comes in." The resulting Tramway Gas Station, with its spectacular wingspan roof cantilevering out over the desert floor, was the welcoming beacon to travelers approaching Palm Springs that the City Council had hoped for.

Because the unique concept he had in mind was difficult to visualize from drawings Frey made a small scale model of the modernist service station for council approval and to help facilitate the necessary permits. Once these hurdles were passed construction began on the 2,300-sq.ft. building. Cement blocks, which Frey had sandblasted to bring out the hidden aggregate colors, formed the base of the building and were horizontally offset to create a textured effect around the curving walls of the Station.

The dramatic roof is a 95-foot-long hyperbolic paraboloid constructed of ribbed galvanized steel panels set on steel beams. This soaring metal canopy with a shorter wing at the other end, is supported by six slender pipe columns and is the key design element of the ingenious building. When it was completed the Station was occupied by

The dramatic roof is a 95-foot-long sweep of ribbed galvanized steel panels set on steel beams.

ENCO, an affiliate of Humble Oil, and became a familiar sight to travelers along th windy stretch of Highway 111 leading into Palm Springs.

In the 1970s and 1980s an economic downturn hit the Coachella Valley and bus nesses, including the Tramway Gas Station, suffered as a result. By the early 1990s th Station was closed, boarded up, and soon tagged with graffiti. In 1996 a private deve oper bought the Station with the intention of demolishing it and subdividing the lan into parcels for a tract of houses. Community protest caused the City Council to desig nate the building a "class one historic site," which would block alterations without th City's approval. The owner objected and at the next Council meeting the designatio was reversed. However, the developer's plans fell through and by 1998 the derelic Tramway Gas Station was back on the market.

It was saved from the wrecking ball by a pair of San Francisco businessmen wh read about the endangered structure and its aerodynamic flying-wedge roofline in a article in *The New Yorker* magazine. They bought the property in 1998 and began restoration process to convert the property into an upscale art and sculpture galler

The roof in the form of a hyperbolic paraboloid —despite its sweeping geometry—
could be built with straight steel beams.

consulting with Albert Frey shortly before his death to bring the Station back as closely as possible to his original vision. The gallery opened early in 2000, and the City Council once again designated the building as a "class one historic site." In December, 2002, the city of Palm Springs purchased the building for $638,000 and budgeted another $500,000 for a restoration that included an extensive remodeling of the building's interior, drought-resistant landscaping, a new parking lot, and the addition of a separate building for restroom facilities. In November, 2003, Frey's iconic Tramway Gas Station was reopened as the official City of Palm Springs Visitors' Center.

Life and Work

Albert Frey in November 1931 at the roof terrace of the Aluminaire

Albert Frey in the late sixties on the Tramway Mountain Station

1903 ▶ Albert Frey, Jr. born to Albert and Ida Frey in Zurich, Switzerland, October 18.

1922–1924 ▶ Attends Institute of Technology in Winterthur, Switzerland and apprentices with Zurich architect A. J. Arter.

1924 ▶ Graduates and travels to Italy for a holiday.

1925 ▶ In September moves to Brussels to pursue his interest in modern architecture. Works there for Jean-Jules Eggericx and Raphaël Verwilghen, a firm active in the modern movement.

1927 ▶ In February moves home to Zurich in order to save money to go to Paris. Works for Leuenberger und Flückiger on traditional cooperative housing and competitions.

1928 ▶ In October travels to Paris. Goes to work at the atelier of Le Corbusier and Pierre Jeanneret. Applies for a United States visa.

1928–1929 ▶ Works with Le Corbusier on the Villa Savoye, Centrosoyus Administration Building, Moscow, Villa Church, and other projects.

1929 ▶ Returns to Brussels and the office of Eggericx and Verwilghen.

1930 ▶ In September arrives in New York and finds work with A. Lawrence Kocher, architect and managing editor of *Architectural Record*.

1930–1931
Aluminaire, Syosset, NY

1931 ▶ Works part-time for William Lescaze.
Chrystie-Forsyth Street Housing Development (project)
Dodge office furniture (project)
Downyflake Donut shop (project)
Farmhouse "A" and "B" (project)

1932 ▶ Cross-country trip by car to meet with and see the work of Frank Lloyd Wright, Richard Neutra, Rudolf M. Schindler, Julius Ralph Davidson and Kem Weber. Aluminaire represents the American modern movement at the "International Exhibition of Modern Architecture" at the Grand Central Palace in New York.
Experimental Five Room House (project)
Experimental Weekend House (project)
Ralph-Barbarin House, Stamford, CT

1933
Gut-Frey House, Zurich, Switzerland

1934 ▶ From January to March moves to Washington, D.C. to work on the Farm Housing Project for the U.S. Department of Agriculture. Resumes Kocher and Frey partnership.
Kocher Canvas Weekend House, Northport, NY

1934–1935
Kocher-Samson Building, Palm Springs, CA

1935
Guthrie House, Palm Springs, CA
San Jacinto Hotel, Palm Springs, CA

1935–1937 ▶ Dissolves partnership with A. Lawrence Kocher and moves to Palm Springs. Works with John Porter Clark.

1936
La Siesta Court, Palm Springs, CA

1937 ▶ Returns to New York to work as contributing designer with Philip L. Goodwin and Edward Durell Stone on the Museum of Modern Art.

1938 ▶ Marries Marian Cook in New York. They divorce in 1945.
Swiss Pavillion, New York World's Fair, 1939 (project) in collaboration with A. Lawrence Kocher

1939 ▶ Publishes *In Search of A Living Architecture*. Cross-country road trip to Palm Springs, stopping to visit with Frank Lloyd Wright. Resumes partnership with John Porter Clark.

1940
Frey House I (Remolding 1953), Palm Springs, CA
Elementary School, Cathedral City, CA

1941
Cahuilla Elementary School, Palm Springs, CA
Palm Springs City Gates, Palm Springs, CA

Palm Springs Water Company, Palm Springs, CA
Markham House, Smoke Tree Ranch, Palm Springs, CA
F.D. Johnson House, Smoke Tree Ranch, Palm Springs, CA

1942
American Airlines Terminal, Palm Springs (project)
El Mirador Hotel conversion to Torner Hospital, Palm Springs, CA
Overly House, Smoke Tree Ranch, Palm Springs, CA

1943 ► Receives California architect's license.

1945
Bel Vista War Housing Development, Palm Springs, CA
Cree House I, Palm Springs, CA
Doll House Restaurant, Palm Springs, CA
Hatton House, Palm Springs, CA
Nichols Building, Palm Springs, CA
Racquet Club Bungalows, Palm Springs, CA
Woolley House, Palm Springs, CA

1945–1947
Villa Hermosa, Palm Springs, CA

1946
Elementary School, Desert Hot Springs, CA
Samson Office Building, Palm Springs, CA
Seeburg Building, Palm Springs, CA

1946–1947
Loewy House, Palm Springs, CA

1947
Clark and Frey Office Building, Palm Springs, CA
Cree Ranch House, Palm Springs, CA (project)
Dollard Office Building, Palm Springs, CA
Paddock Pool Company Office Warehouse Building, Palm Springs, CA
San Gorgonio Pass Memorial Hospital, Banning, CA

1948
American Legion Post #519, Palm Springs, CA
Desert Bank, Palm Springs, CA
El Mirador Hotel Restoration, Palm Springs, CA

Lyons House, Smoke Tree Ranch, Palm Springs, CA
Turner House, Smoke Tree Ranch, Palm Springs, CA

1948–1949
Katherine Finchy Elementary School, Palm Springs, CA

1949
Vista Colorado Elementary School, Needles, CA

1949–1963
Palm Springs Tramway Valley Station, Palm Springs, CA

1950
Benoist Guest House, Palm Springs, CA
Desert Hospital, Palm Springs, CA
Palm Springs Fire Station, Palm Springs, CA
University of California at Riverside Social Sciences & Humanities Building, Riverside, CA

1951
Dollard House, Rancho Mirage, CA
Parker Dam School, Needles, CA
Pelletier House, Palm Desert, CA

1952 ► Robson C. Chambers made partner and firm name changed to Clark, Frey & Chambers
Cahuilla Elementary School Multi-Purpose Building, Palm Springs, CA

1952–1957
City Hall, Palm Springs, CA

1953
Palm Springs Desert Museum, Palm Springs, CA
Nichols Building (other buildings), Palm Springs, CA

1954
Banning Library, Banning, CA
Hinton House, La Jolla, CA

1955 ► July and August, Frey goes on a trip around the world.
Cielo Vista School, Palm Springs, CA
Fire Station #1, Palm Springs, CA

1955–1956
Cree House II, Cathedral City, CA

1956 ► John Porter Clark leaves firm.
Carey House, Palm Springs, CA
First Church of Christ, Palm Springs, CA

1957 ► Frey designated FAIA.
Foursquare Gospel Church, Palm Springs, CA

1957–1958
Première Apartments, Palm Springs, CA

1958
Saint Michael's By-The-Sea Episcopal Church, Carlsbad, CA

1958–1959
North Shore Yacht Club, Salton Sea, CA

1959
American Red Cross Chapter House, Riverside, CA
North Shore Beach Estates (project), Salton Sea, CA
North Shore Beach Motel (altered), Salton Sea, CA

1960
Alpha Beta Food Market, Indio, CA
Alpha Beta Food Market, Palm Springs, CA
Monkey Tree Motel (altered), Palm Springs, CA

1963–1964
Frey House II, Palm Springs, CA

1963–1965
Tramway Gas Station, Palm Springs, CA

1964
F. E. Supple House, Smoke Tree Ranch, Palm Springs, CA
Armstrong House, Smoke Tree Ranch, Palm Springs, CA
Post Office, Blythe, CA

1965
Shell Oil Company, Palm Springs, CA

1966 ► Robson C. Chambers leaves Frey and Chambers. From the late 1960s until his death in 1998, Frey was semi-retired, working out of his

Palm Springs

ome-office. He was selective in his projects,
vhich included residential commissions and
onsultations on the restoration and alteration of
is earlier work, much of it for later generations
t Smoke Tree Ranch.

990 ▶ Frey archive acquired by University of
California at Santa Barbara Art Museum
Architectural Drawing Collection.

992 ▶ Exhibition titled "Albert Frey: Modern
Architect" at UCSB Art Museum opens in March,
nd at the Palm Springs Desert Museum in
eptember.

993 ▶ "Albert Frey: Modern Architect" opens
n March at the Columbia University School of
Architecture.

995 ▶ "Albert Frey: Modern Architect" travels to
ree venues in Switzerland: Architekturmuseum
asel in February; EPF Lausanne, Department of
rchitecture in May; and ETH Zurich, Institut gta,
n October.

98 ▶ November 14, Frey passes away of natural
auses at home in Frey House II.

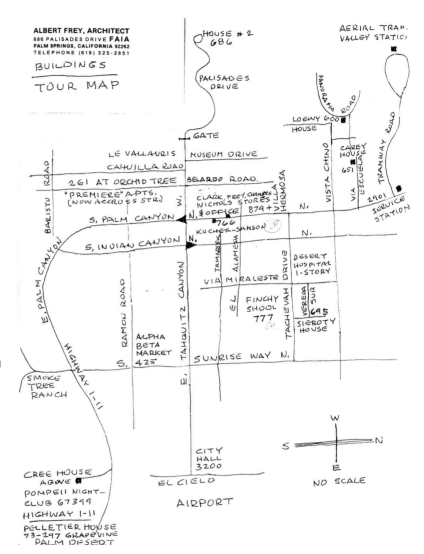

Bibliography

Credits

The Author

▶ Anderson, Kurt. *Annals of Architecture: Desert Cool*. The New Yorker, Feb 22, 1998.
▶ Banham, Reyner. *The Architecture of the Well-Tempered Environment*. London: The Architectural Press, 1969.
▶ Cygelman, Adele. *Palm Springs Modern*. New York: Rizzoli, 1999.
▶ Frey, Albert and Kocher, Lawrence. *Real Estate Subdivisions for Low-Cost Housing*. Architectural Record, April, 1931.
▶ Frey, Albert. *In Search of A Living Architecture*. New York: Architectural Book Publishing Company, Inc., 1939.
▶ Gebhard, David and Winter, Robert. *A Guide to Architecture in Los Angeles and Southern California*. Salt Lake City: Peregrine Smith, 1977.
▶ Goldberger, Paul. *Icon of Modernism Poised for Extinction*. The New York Times, March, 1987.
▶ Golub, Jennifer. *Albert Frey: Houses 1 + 2*. New York: Princeton Architectural Press, 1999.
▶ Hess, Alan and Danish, Andrew. *Palm Springs Weekend*. San Francisco: Chronicle Books, 2001.
▶ Hitchcock, Henry-Russell and Johnson, Philip. *The International Style: Arch Since 1922*. New York: WW Norton Company, 1932.
▶ Jackson, Neil. *The Modern Steel House*. London: Chapman Hall, 1996.
▶ Loewy, Raymond. *Never Leave Well Enough Alone*. New York: Simon and Schuster, 1950.
▶ Rosa, Joseph. *Albert Frey, architect*. New York: Rizzoli, 1990.
▶ *A House for the Sickened World*. Casabella, December, 1999.
▶ *Albert Frey, Frey House 2, Palm Springs*. GA Houses 40, 1994.
▶ *Architectural Show Has First Zipper House*. New York Herald Tribune, April 19, 1931.
▶ *Canvas For Houses*. Architectural Forum, December, 1932.
▶ *Designed for Multi-Stage Construction*. Architectural Record, January, 1953.
▶ *Elementary School: Palm Springs, California*. Progressive Architecture, July, 1963.
▶ *House, Palm Springs, California*. Progressive Architecture, July, 1948.
▶ *New Architecture Elements*. Architectural Forum, September, 1942.
▶ *Two Desert Houses in Palm Springs, California*. Arts & Architecture, July, 1945.

Gloria Koenig is an architectural historian and the author of *Charles & Ray Eames: Pioneers of Mid-Century Modernism*; *Iconic LA: Stories of LA's Most Memorable Buildings*, and *Nature's Architects: The Evolution of Design*. She has published and lectured widely on a variety of topics in contemporary architecture, and served as consultant with filmmakers on a documentary about her late husband, modernist architect Pierr Koenig.